Eugene MAGALIF

Romance
for Flute and Piano

To Rita D'Arcangelo

To Rita D'Arcangelo

ROMANCE

**Eugene Magalif,
ASCAP**

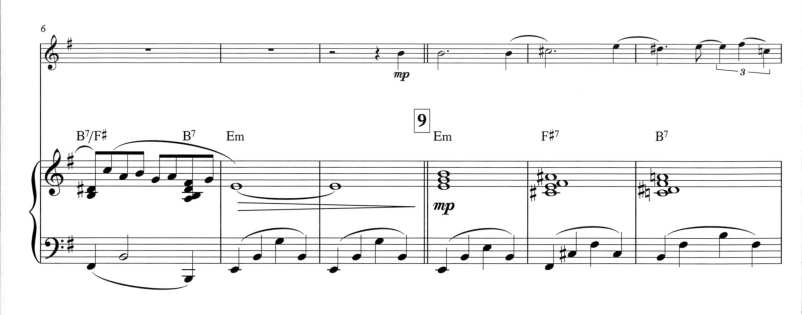

Eugene MAGALIF

Romance
for Flute and Piano

To Rita D'Arcangelo

Flute

To Rita D'Arcangelo
ROMANCE

Eugene Magalif,
ASCAP

Flute

3

SOUTHERN MUSIC FLUTE WORKS
SELECTED FLUTE EDITIONS/ ARRANGEMENTS

COLLECTIONS

Nancy Andrews
Paris Conservatory Album: 16 Short Lyric Pieces — B579 - HL240976
Gilbert and Sullivan, arr. Galway/ Overton
Arias for Flute and Piano — B577 - HL240978
Arias for Flute Choir — B583 - HL240979
Arias for Two Flutes and Piano — B584 - HL240981

SOLOS (with piano accompaniment unless otherwise stated)

Giulio Briccialdi, arr. Sir James Galway
The Carnival of Venice (Il Carnevale di Venezia) — SU797 - HL240977
Eugene Magalif
For Tanya (opt. Flute 2 and Wind Chimes) — SU810 - HL244914
Eugene Magalif
Romance — SU811 - HL244916
Eugene Magalif
Revelation — SU809 - HL244915
Jules Mouquet, ed. Sir James Galway
La Flute de Pan — SU804 - HL240982
Johann Quantz, ed. Sir James Galway
Concerto in G Major — SU805 - HL240983
M.A. Reichert, arr. Sir James Galway
The Encore Solo (unaccompanied) — SU794 - HL240984
Paul Taffanel, ed. Sir James Galway
Grand Fantasy on Mignon — SU795 - HL240985
Paul Wetzger, arr. Sir James Galway
Am Waldesbach (By the Forest Brook), Op. 33 — SU798 - HL240986
Charles-Marie Widor, ed. Sir James Galway
Suite — SU803 - HL240987

Southern MUSIC

EXCLUSIVELY DISTRIBUTED BY
HAL•LEONARD®

keisersouthernmusic.com
Questions/ comments? info@southernmusic.com

LA RONDE DES LUTINS
(*Dance of the Goblins*)
for Violin and Piano

Violin

Critical Urtext Edition
Edited by Endre Granat

ANTONIO BAZZINI, Op. 25

EDITOR'S NOTE

A protégé of Niccolo Paganini, Antonio Bazzini (1818-1897) began his career as a highly successful virtuoso violinist, concertizing all over Europe. He was amongst the first violinists who did not exclusively perform his own composition but also masterpieces of the past and those of his contemporaries. Accompanied on the piano by the composer, Bazzini gave the premier performance of the e minor Violin Concerto by Mendelssohn for an invited audience.

1864 Bazzini returned to Italy to devote his life to composition. As Professor of Composition at the Milan Conservatory he taught both Mascagni and Puccini.

Most of Bazzini's compositions are forgotten. "LA RONDE DES LUTINS" is the only work that has not lost its popularity. This great bravura piece uses many of Paganini 's innovations, ricochet and flying staccato bowings, double harmonics, left hand pizzicato, and repetition of the same pitch on all four strings.

This work remained one of Jascha Heifetz' favorite encores. He recorded "La Ronde des Lutins" in 1917 and again in 1937. His bowings, fingerings and his suggestions regarding interpretation are integral part of this edition.

Endre Granat

8

6

10

The HEIFETZ Collection for Violin

This exclusive series of Jascha Heifetz violin editions includes wonderful arrangements and transcriptions from Heifetz's own manuscripts. Our world-class editors Endre Granat and Stephen Shipps have taken these hidden treasures to painstakingly produce these new performance and Urtext Critical editions.

HANDEL PASSACAGLIA FOR TWO VIOLINS *ed. Stephen Shipps/ Endre Granat*

Outside of his native Norway, Johan Halvorsen (1864-1935) is known internationally only for his arrangement of Handel's Harpsichord Suite. The Passacaglia is performed as a mainstay of Duo programs in his arrangements for both Violin/Cello and Violin/Viola. Jascha Heifetz established these duos in the standard literature by playing and recording countless performances with William Primrose and Gregor Piatigorsky.
HL001265549—S511002

WIENIAWSKI POLONAISE BRILLANTE NO. 1 (Polonaise de Concert) *ed. Endre Granat*

In 1848, the thirteen year old Henryk Wieniawski wrote the first sketches to his Polonaise in D major. The composition was published in Germany in 1853 as *Polonaise de Concert in D major op. 4*. When the work was re-published in Paris (1858), the title changed to "Polonaise Brillante". Tremendously popular already during the composer's life time, this work has been on the repertory of virtually every virtuoso violinist ever since. This new Critical Urtext Edition corrects obvious misprints while keeping the format of the 1853 first edition, printing the textural changes on the Paris version as foot notes.
HL001414930—S511020

WIENIAWSKI POLONAISE BRILLANTE NO. 2 *ed. Endre Granat*

Completed at the zenith of Wieniawski's career in 1869, this virtuoso piece showcases the playing of many fast, short and accented notes on one bow stroke which came to be called the "Wieniawski staccato". The slow midsection in F major contains some of Wieniawski's most lyrical themes while double stops and trills conclude this irresistible work. The signed and dated (1869) manuscript found its home in the library of Jascha Heifetz. As a member of Mr. Heifetz's studio, editor Endre Granat studied this work with the Master. This Critical Urtext Edition is based on this manuscript and the first printed edition (Schott 1875).
HL001265550—S511019

SAINT-SAËNS INTRODUCTION AND RONDO CAPRICCIOSO *ed. Endre Granat*

This work was originally intended to be the rousing Finale to Saint-Saëns' First Violin Concerto, op.20. Saint-Saëns' favorite violinist Pablo de Sarasate gave the first performance in 1867 in Paris with the composer conducting. In 1869 Saint-Saëns entrusted his younger colleague Georges Bizet to create a reduction of the orchestra score for Violin and Piano. The composer's autograph score and the first edition of the work were the primary source material for this publication.
HL001414931—S511021

SAINT-SAËNS HAVANAISE, OP. 83 *ed. Endre Granat*

The composer dedicated this work which dates from 1885-87 to Rafael Diaz Albertini, a violinist of Cuban origin. This Critical Urtext Edition is based on the composer's manuscript, the first print of the violin and piano version, and to a large part, on the historic recording by the composer himself with the violinist Gabriel Willaume (1919).
HL001414932—S511012

THE JASCHA HEIFETZ BEETHOVEN FOLIO *ed. Endre Granat*

Contains Heifetz' *Three Cadenzas to the Beethoven Concerto for Violin and Orchestra in D Major op.61*, along with the Beethoven violin solo with piano version, *Turkish March op. 113* and *Chorus of the Dervishes op.113*, both from *The Ruins on Athens*. All works in the collection are Critical Urtext Editions by Endre Granat.
HL001145437—S511024

BAZZINI LA RONDE DES LUTINS (DANCE OF THE GOBLINS) CRITICAL URTEXT EDITION *ed. Endre Granat*

This great bravura piece uses many of the innovations the composer learned from his teacher, Niccolo Paganini--ricochet and flying staccato bowings, double harmonics, left hand pizzicato, and repetition of the same pitch on all four strings. This work remained one of Jascha Heifetz' favorite encores. He recorded it in 1917 and again in 1937. His bowings, fingerings and his suggestions regarding interpretation are integral part of this edition.
HL001533335—S511025

PAGANINI WITCHES DANCE (LE STREGHE) FOR VIOLIN AND PIANO OP. 8, CRITICAL URTEXT EDITION *ed. Endre Granat*

A mature work of Paganini, Witches Dance uses all the innovations he had introduced as a violin virtuoso performer. Like so many of his other works, it was not published during the composer's lifetime. Jascha Heifetz' bowings, fingerings and suggestions regarding interpretation are an integral part of this Critical Urtext edition by Endre Granat.
HL001533336—S511026